D0741918

SIGHTINGS

in the Valley of the Shadow

Reflections
on Dying

Balfour M. Mount

Foreword by
Joseph Bayly

InterVarsity Press
Downers Grove
Illinois 60515

To M. H. M. and H. T. R. M.

I wish to acknowledge my indebtedness and gratitude for assistance and support to my family, Mr. Tom Daly, Dr. Ina Ajemian and Dr. John Scott. Sincere thanks to Ms. Susan Smythe and Mrs. Edith Boltz for their tireless efforts in preparing the manuscript and photographs respectively. Grateful thanks to Professor Louis Dudek of McGill University and May Ebbett Cutler, Montreal, for their editorial advice.

InterVarsity Press is the book-publishing division of Inter-Varsity Christian Fellowship, a student movement active on campus at hundreds of universities, colleges and schools of nursing. For information about local and regional activities, write IVCF, 233 Langdon St., Madison, WI 53703.

Distributed in Canada through InterVarsity Press, 860 Denison St., Unit 3, Markham, Ontario L3R 4H1, Canada.

All quotations from the Scriptures are from the Revised Standard Version of the Bible, copyrighted 1946, 1952, © *1971, 1973 by the Division of Christian Education of the National Council of the Churches of Christ in the USA, and used by permission.*

Cover photograph: Gary Irving

ISBN 0-87784-807-6

Printed in the United States of America

Library of Congress Cataloging in Publication Data

Mount, Balfour M.
    Sightings.

    1. Consolation.   2. Death–Religious aspects–Christianity. I. Title.
BV4905.2.M69 1983   242'.4   83-302
ISBN 0-87784-807-6

17	16	15	14	13	12	11	10	9	8	7	6	5	4	3	2	1
97	96	95	94	93	92	91	90	89	88	87	86	85	84	83		

Foreword

This book is a sensitive study of dying by a superbly
qualified professional. But it is not detached, dispas-
sionate.

It could not be: the professional is watching his mother
die, is saying farewells, sharing feelings, asking
questions. This is poetry, not a case study.

The author's photographs add a dimension of realism,
open a frosted window so that we may see the event more
clearly—through his eyes as well as through his mind.

We also see it through his spirit. This is a Christian
perspective on death and dying. Hope pervades pain,
faith incites hope. To say that the book is Christian
is not to limit it to the persuaded; rather, its sharply
defined focus enlarges the field to all who suffer, grieve
and fear death.

The author, Balfour Mount, M.D., is the leader of
Canada's death awareness movement. Dr. Mount
established the first palliative care center, similar to
the hospice concept, at the Royal Victoria Hospital in
Montreal. Behind the sensitivity of this book and Dr.
Mount's penetrating insights are his own successful battle
with cancer years ago as a young intern and his fellowship at St. Christopher's Hospice in London where
Dr. Cicely Saunders was his mentor.

I met Balfour Mount's mother once, about twenty years ago, at a Christian Medical Society conference in New England. Her stately dignity impressed me; so did her wisdom and warmth, especially toward the other—all younger—wives. Even though my acquaintance was limited to that conference, I recognize the same wise, dignified lady in this book. That was also the time I met her distinguished neurosurgeon husband and their son.

Over the intervening years I have come to consider Bal Mount a friend. We have participated together in death and dying seminars; more significantly, we have revealed some burdens and joys of living to each other.

Like another Friend, Dr. Mount is "acquainted with grief." In these sensitive and creative meditations he shares that acquaintance to our great benefit.

Joseph Bayly
Bartlett, Illinois

MAUDE HENRY MOUNT

Introduction

"How do you prepare to die, Bal? How do you?" Her eyes filled with tears. She leaned forward, her face betraying the well of tension and controlled urgency within. Her abdomen was distended. She had learned the results of the liver scan only the day before. Her liver was now filled with metastases from her bowel cancer.

She had always radiated a dynamic energy that was other-person oriented. She had always directed attention and conversation away from herself, away from her feelings toward those of others. Now all was changed. Her own needs overwhelmed her. For the first time in my memory Mother gave vent to her own anguish. Our eyes met. Surely this could not be happening. Surely it was inconceivable that this vital spirit should die! It was June 2, 1980.

My parents had arrived by bus from Ottawa in the late afternoon. After dinner we had strolled to the nearby school yard so that my nine-year-old son could show his grandparents his baseball skills. With customary flair Mother said, "Here, let me see that bat for a moment." Then with ease and great skill she flipped the softball into the air and slugged it soundly out onto the playground with the quip, "I used to be the best baseball player in Springfield."

"Come on now, bet you couldn't do that again."

There followed a steady stream of hits deep into the outfield. She never missed. Mother's age was uncertain but she was known to be over eighty.

After returning home she had joked that the various pieces of orthopedic hardware from previous surgical exploits might prove awkward for a small urn after cremation. As the quiet of evening settled, however, her deep questioning surfaced. In the lengthening shadows, Mother, Dad and I sat and talked. She was a person earnestly trying to find comfort in the face of desolation.

There was a pause, then, "I don't fear dying. I don't feel anything. I don't know what I think. I guess it's over. And I guess that's all right. Yet I worry about Harry."

Maude Henry was born in the closing years of the nineteenth century. She never would disclose the exact date of her birth, preferring to let her air of perennial youth convey her "age."

Second youngest of four children born to a prosperous merchant in a small Ontario town, she combined intelligence, carefree good looks, energy and a sparkling sense of humor with an abundance of ambition.

While still in her teens she qualified as a teacher, briefly threw herself into one-room schoolhouse teaching, then set her sights on a nursing career. Characteristically, her adventuresome spirit carried her not to a local Canadian nursing program but to St. Luke's Hospital in New York City.

In 1925 she married Harry Telford Roy Mount, an earnest young Canadian surgeon. Their life together was a kaleidoscope of rich experiences combining two complex and powerful personalities, a testimonial to both the Protestant work ethic and dedication to family.

At their fiftieth wedding anniversary they could look back on a wealth of treasured memories. They had thrived in the harsh conditions of northern Newfoundland and Labrador as they worked with Sir Wilfred Grenfell and his medical team at the Grenfell Mission. Tales told of "mug-ups" at the side of the trail as they traveled by dog team between isolated fishing villages, and surgery carried out in the primitive surroundings of a fishing cabin.

Training at the Mayo Clinic was followed by a long and productive surgical career in Ottawa, including the development of neurosurgery in that city. There also followed a family: Jim, Alice and Balfour.

Now malignancy. Progressive in the face of repeated surgery. Spread to the liver. A variety of images crowded my mind as I recalled Mother's impact on all around her. Mother had tolerated my father's preoccupation with his patients and a career of service. She had almost single-handedly molded home and children with intense interest and devotion.

She added determination, spice, flair and a dash of

irreverence to all she touched. She was an original.

The episode of the stubborn neighbor perhaps illustrates the point. It wasn't that she bore our new neighbor any ill will! Indeed, she had been determined to reach out in welcome when it became clear that the vacant lot beside our house was to be the site of a new home. The chain of events that followed, however, gradually eroded her charitable resolve.

First there was the matter of the fence. City bylaws were ignored as the excavations for the new house extended to our property line, toppling our fence and adjacent trees. Inquiries met with a municipal deaf ear. Our new neighbor, Mr. G., was indifferent. Mother's jaw became more firmly set. Yet she remained determined to be hospitable. The final test was yet to come.

Several months after the neighbors moved in, fate smiled in a singularly ironic way. For whatever reason the telephone company, in their wisdom, changed many telephone numbers. Soon our phone, already heavily in demand to handle the calls from my father's patients, became even busier. The new calls were for a local cleaning establishment whose old telephone number we now possessed. We were informed by one frustrated customer that the phone number appeared on the cleaners' stationery and statements of account. The owner of the business was our new neighbor!

What to do? The phone company refused to change the number. The girls at the cleaners were sympathetic but said they could do nothing without Mr. G's permission. Mother called him and, after identifying herself, carefully explained her plight. She was pleasant, almost apologetic. His response was swift and blunt. He had just had a large supply of stationery printed, and we

would have to put up with the inconvenience until it had
all been used.

"But surely you could have the girls simply change the
phone number as the account is made out," Mother
calmly suggested.

"It would waste too much of their time."

"Surely it must be harmful for business to have your
customers so inconvenienced."

"That's my business," came the retort.

Mother was polite and controlled as she hung up the
phone. She looked determined. I had seen that look before.

As I recall, the matter was not discussed further. It
was the next afternoon, I believe, when the phone rang
and Mother cheerily called, "I'll get it." I was dumb-
founded when the pause following her usually bright
"hello" was broken by a rather brassy, "What's that, lady?
Just a second, I can't hear a thing around here with all
these boilers going." Then, holding the phone away from
her, "Hey Ralph, some old biddy here calling about
her husband's shirts!" Then into the receiver, "Sorry,
lady, you'll have to call back. Maybe tomorrow."

On the next call, an irate customer was demanding
a dress shirt that was needed without delay. "Listen,
Mister," intoned Mother airily, "you'll be lucky if we
find that shirt by this time next week."

The third call was to dispute a bill. "Don't worry about
a thing, lady," was Mother's comment. "I am sure we
overcharged you. Just don't pay the bill."

All calls stopped within forty-eight hours! The twinkle
in Mother's eye lasted considerably longer.

Mother dying. We had faced death as a family before.
I remember as a child waiting apprehensively in the
hospital corridor. Mother was experiencing postsurgical

complications that endangered her life. A few years
later my father and I narrowly escaped death in the crash
of a private plane. As an intern I had developed cancer
and required radical surgery, chemotherapy and irradia-
tion. Then, as we adjusted to the probability of my death,
we were subjected to a whirlwind of crises, a series of
encounters with our finite nature. My brother's talented
young wife, then in her late twenties, died in childbirth.
I developed a neck mass that required further surgery.
My sister, expecting her second child in England, had
a life-threatening antepartum hemorrhage. My wife and
our newborn son developed serious complications following his birth. In these experiences we learned something about the numbing effect of life lived in crisis, about
the apparent senselessness of much human suffering,
and about God's willingness to provide comfort in times
of strife.

As I confronted the possibility of Mother's death,
other factors colored my perception. My professional
career had shifted recently from surgical oncology, which
involved me in radical cancer surgery, giving chemotherapy and carrying out animal research, to a new interest, the care of the terminally ill.

In 1973 we had studied the experiences of dying cancer
patients and their families at the Royal Victoria Hospital
in Montreal. The Palliative Care Service was established
in 1975 to correct the unacceptable deficiencies we
had uncovered. In my new career I was privileged to sit
with many dying patients both at the hospice and at
St. Christopher's Hospice in England. Now the tables were
turned. Now I was the family member, not the doctor.
As I contemplated the possibility of Mother's death, and as
the mind-wrenching reality of it took form, I was filled

with the questions I had so frequently discussed with others. No longer theoretical. No longer them. Her. Us. Me. I challenged the standard answers. I remembered the words on a poster hanging in our church's teen room: "If you have all the answers, you haven't asked all the questions."

"Why do the young die? Why does anybody die? Tell me." Zorba the Greek's question came home with fresh urgency.

"If God is God he is not good. If God is good he is not God." The problem of reconciling unmerited suffering with an all-powerful good God, so succinctly stated in these words by Archibald MacLeish in his play *J. B.*, found a new depth of meaning as I looked at Mother's face.

If we but have faith we can achieve anything, move mountains, be cured!

What will happen to her after she is gone? Is there *really* anything after death?

I realized that these questions filled not only my mind but hers as well. They filled my father's mind and pre-occupied others in our family. Often they went unexpressed. Too painful to discuss her impending death. Too morbid.

As a professional I knew her mind was teeming. I knew the benefits to be accrued through expressing fears. She was nearly frantic with the overwhelming urgency of these questions, with the immensity of their implications. As a son, I found them difficult to discuss.

Her birthday was approaching. August 14, 1980. It would be her last. What could I give her? She had no need for material things. The answer came one evening as we sat chatting. She was weak, depressed. While she was anxious to project calm, it was clear she was in turmoil.

"Bal, I have more questions than answers. I thought I had a faith. Now I'm not sure. I wish I had someone or something to minister to these needs. Something to read." I knew what to give. "On Learning to Trust," the first piece that follows, was written the next day.

Following the family party on August 14, Mother retired to the living room to lie down. Her face was drawn with fatigue and the discomfort in her abdomen. The tumor had taken its toll. Weakness consumed. In these moments of privacy I read my offering to her. Dad joined us. We shared; touched; cried.

The days that followed were supercharged with questioning, with meaning, with concern, with suffering. The prose and photographs in this book evolved as two avenues of expression of all that we experienced in that unmerciful pressure cooker. For me, they proved to be rivers of relief, helpful outlets for channeling feelings. The daily writings evolved in response to the questions raised in our discussions. They seemed to help her. They facilitated our discussions. They made it easier to talk about painful issues, a fact that helped each of us.

The photography arose for another reason. I had become involved in photography during my visit to St. Christopher's Hospice. As a surgeon, my misgivings about putting dying persons together were so marked that I felt that if it *were* a good idea, I would have to document that fact in pictures. I borrowed a camera. Those first photographs of excellence in terminal care, of questioning faces, of the experiences and feelings in that British haven, helped to sell the Royal Victory Hospital on the concept of hospice care. And it involved me in photography as a means of expressing the deeply important moments of the last days of living.

Mother, always previously reticent about having her picture taken, seemed to want to leave a legacy—for her loved ones. Fast film was used so that there was no flash. My picture taking was only briefly discussed with her and the other members of the family. The photographs were to be a private record of a watershed event in our lives.

In the weeks before death the flow of questions continued. So did the writings. We read them together, or they were read to her by my father. The biblical passages they contained were circled and read separately at her request when she was tired. These jottings became a focus of sharing for the three of us.

Following her death we were wrapped in the cotton-wool sense of unreality so common to the bereaved. The questions and depth of feeling continued, as did the help experienced in committing them to paper.

Sometime after Mother's death the writings and photographs were shown to three friends: Dr. Ina Ajemian and Dr. John Scott, the two physicians whose dedication had made the Palliative Care Service possible, and Tom Daly, a gifted film maker from Canada's National Film Board whose sensitive film *The Last Days of Living* so profoundly depicts the experiences of our service. It was on their urging that the visual and written outpourings of those weeks are now shared with others. It was their feeling that, although they were written from a Christian perspective, they would speak to people from other religious traditions.

Arising as they did out of the intensity of the moment and my discussions and reflections in those pressured days, the writings tend to focus on the issues before us from the highly personal perspective of the son-mother relationship I was involved in. What they unfortunately fail to convey is the rich texture of the relationships that each of the other family members had with Mother and with the others in the family. It was a shared event. One can only regret this limitation and hope that the photographs help to dispel this note of exclusiveness.

Because of the events and feelings involved, these private archives are opened with some misgiving. They are not offered with a sense that they settle issues, answer questions or quell doubts, but with the hope that they may crystallize and stimulate thought, bring a measure of comfort, and break down barriers to discussion that are frequently experienced by those of us who find ourselves standing with our loved ones in the arena of death.

1 On Learning to Trust

14 August 1980
Ottawa

How do you prepare to die? you asked.
We are caught, pinned, held motionless in the invisible
    vice of our destiny
Face to face with reality
Unforgiving in its harshness. *We are finite.*
We are dazed—suspended in time and space.

Has it been life—*Life*—Mother? It has been I know. For,
    it is in giving that we receive and *how* you have given!
    Your outward stance fiercely giving—to family.
        Defending. Always defending family—
                            against others
                            against each other
                            against ourselves
    (too much perhaps, and we to pay the price).
Always there,
Always supporting us in our hours of need.

This is *your* hour of need, Mother.
How can I support you?
How can I bear you up in my arms?
How can I fend off the foe, protect you?

We are Helpless,
        Naked,
            Vulnerable,
                Uncertain.   We are essentially alone!
                            Darkness is all around us.
But in these moments of breathless anguish

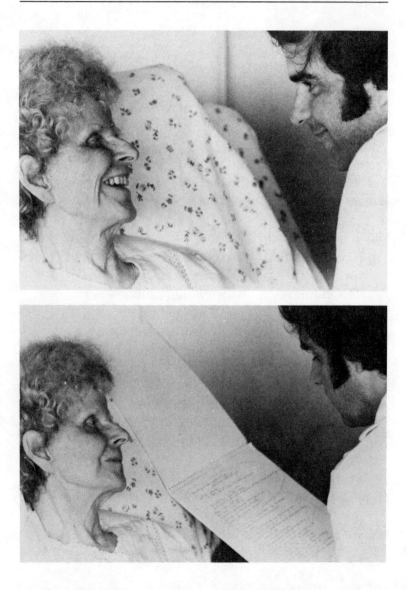

we are opened
we pause—long enough to hear
    in the stillness, a voice
"Come unto me all ye who labor and are heavy laden
    and I will give you rest."

"Let not your hearts be troubled;
Believe in God, believe also in me.
In my Father's house are many rooms;
If it were not so,
Would I have told you that I go to prepare a place for you?
And when I go and prepare a place for you,
I will come again and will take you to myself,
That where I am you may be also."
_____

In our pain we question God.
How can it be?
We doubt his love
            his presence
            his existence.
"If God is God he is not good. If God is good he is not God!"
Answer that God!
Let's hear your answer to that!
_____

And we see a mountaintop
An old man with knife drawn—poised to strike—
    a torch held in his left hand.
On the pile of wood before him—that terrible altar of life—
    lies a boy bound hand and foot.
Stop Time.
Abraham! You follow with such blind faith!
But, what kind of God are you following?
What kind of God is it that would say,

"Take your son, your only son Isaac,
whom you love, and go to the land
of Moriah, and offer him there as a
burnt offering upon one of the mountains
of which I shall tell you"?
You know what? It's just like *life*, God!
You really sock it to us don't you?
You appear to give it all to us,
    only to take it away!
You gave Isaac to Abraham and Sarah in their old age.
A big deal.
Grandstand play.
Benevolent God acts to
    give a son to these two geriatric lovers!
Great miracle.
Laughter. Isn't God great?
    —Then four verses later—
        "And Abraham took the wood of the burnt offering,
        and laid it on Isaac his son;
        and he took in his hand the fire and the knife.
        So they went both of them together."
That beats everything boy!
Isaac the child, not only walking to his death
But having to carry the wood of his own doom
    —Trusting his father.
        Trusting his Father.
Run kid! Don't trust. What kind of God are you?
You know what?
I don't think you are in control of anything.
                            It just happens.
We try to find meaning in this life.
                            It's pathetic.
                            A sordid joke!

You don't exist!
You're a figment of our frustrated human longings!
———

Did you see Isaac's face when he looked up at his father
And asked where the lamb for the offering was?
Did you see it?
So open.
So trusting as he struggled under the burden of
                              his fiery fate.
"God will provide himself the lamb for a burnt offering,
   my son."
Sure have to hand it to you, Abraham—
      That's real faith—
         or senility—
               or perhaps some great mystical turn-on thing.
      Abraham you're an ass!

But then the gasp:
The prophetic nature of Abraham's words,
   spoken in such blind faith,
   sinks in—
   "God will provide himself
      The lamb
      for a
      burnt offering."
What kind of God is this?
What kind of God? we ask.
The kind of God that *did* supply the lamb
      —a Ram, caught in the thicket
         —Isaac's bonds are loosed
               We sigh in wonder and relief.
         —*His* Son, hanging on a cross.
            Our bonds are loosed.

Do we comprehend?
What kind of God is this?
A God that would test Abraham's faith but not demand
    the unthinkable.
Yet, himself, centuries later to offer the unthinkable on
    our behalf.
He offered *His* only Son—for us.
An atonement.
        A ransom.
                Once paid.
                Finally.

————

Those around him were frightened,
                    confused.
He was going to his death.

Why?
Where was God?
What did it mean?
Their questions tumbled out in jumbled agony.
With loving patience Jesus answered them.
   How could he tell them of what was to come?
   How could he explain the cataclysmic
      thing that was about to happen?
   How would they accept his imminent death
      and comprehend the resultant coming
      of the Spirit?
How could they understand, in their hour
      of desolation and fear that God was
      about to give each of them his presence
      in a nature
                        unbounded by human form
                        unrestricted by time and place
      A presence that would be there for each of
      them—for each of those who subsequently, down
      through the ages, would turn to him in their
      hour of need?
How could he explain all this to them?
The oil lamps around the darkened room flickered on their
   worried faces.

He loved them.
Once before, he had seen in them
The fear that now he sensed.
It was that night in the storm
On the Sea of Galilee.
He had been totally spent.
Thinking back
He could feel the ache of the utter fatigue

That had gripped him as he left the multitude
And stepped exhausted into the small boat.
Clouds on the horizon
Everything strangely gripped in an eerie stillness.
Total exhaustion—sleep.
What he later remembered most about the moment
    when he was so rudely awakened, was
    the fear that filled their eyes.
—The same fear that he saw tonight.
—The fear of man confronting death.
"Teacher, do you not care if we perish?"
    The wind and waves
        lashed
      at the boat.
    They were shipping water!
      Instant of terror.
        Stop Time.
He gazed into their troubled eyes.
He saw all humanity.
He saw us in our human frailty as we face our final hour.
    —He saw Dietrich Bonhoeffer lying in the Nazi prison.
    —He saw Martin Luther King facing the angry mob.
    —He saw Maudie lying in a bed, filled with questions
                            filled with uncertainty.
One question flooded his mind—
    "What will sustain all those who come
    through all ages,
    when these my comrades fear, while yet I am with them?
    Even while they touch me
    feel my breath
    they know not
    that death need not be feared.
    What will sustain the others

when my very presence
gives insufficient sustenance
to these fearful ones?"
His question to them
As he turned from the suddenly
Stilled sea
Comes thundering down the centuries.
   "Why are you afraid? Have you no faith?"
—Not faith that the storms of life will all be stilled
—Not faith that God will prevent our suffering
But faith that he is with us *in* our suffering.
Suffering with us.
A suffering God.

All these memories flashed through his mind in that
   upper room.
So much to tell them.
So little time left to them.
So much for them to understand.
And he spoke to them of the meaning of all that was
   happening.
Of his abiding presence.
                A presence that comforted Bonhoeffer
                within those prison walls,
                whence years later he was to say,
                "I believe that God will
                give us all the strength we need to
                help us to resist in all times of distress.
                But he never gives it in advance,
                lest we should rely on ourselves
                and not on him alone."
His gaze fell on each of them in that cloistered room
And then he spoke—to them

—to each of us

"These things I have spoken to you,
   while I am still with you.
But the Counselor,
   the Holy Spirit, whom the Father will send
      in my name,
He will teach you all things,
And bring to your remembrance all that I have said to you.
Peace I leave with you;
My peace I give to you;
Not as the world gives do I give to you.
Let not your hearts be troubled,
Neither let them be afraid.

"I am the true vine, and my Father is the vinedresser.
Every branch of mine that bears no fruit,
He takes away,
And every branch that does bear fruit he prunes,
That it may bear more fruit.
You are already made clean by the word which I have
   spoken to you.
Abide in me, and I in you.
As the branch cannot bear fruit by itself,
Unless it abides in the vine,
Neither can you, unless you abide in me.
I am the vine, you are the branches.
He who abides in me, and I in him,
He it is that bears much fruit,
For apart from me you can do nothing.
If a man does not abide in me,
He is cast forth as a branch and withers;
And the branches are gathered, thrown into the fire
   and burned.

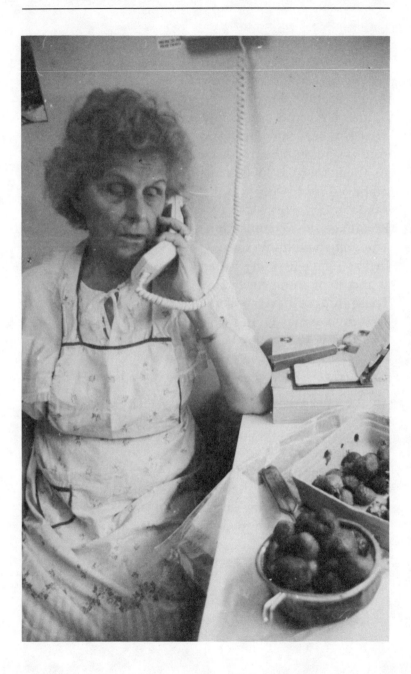

If you abide in me,
And my words abide in you,
Ask whatever you will,
And it shall be done for you.
By this my Father is glorified,
That you bear much fruit,
And so prove to be my disciples.
As the Father has loved me,
So have I loved you;
Abide in my love.
If you keep my commandments,
You will abide in my love,
Just as I have kept my Father's commandments
    and abide in his love.
These things I have spoken to you,
That my *joy* may be in you,
And that your joy may be full!"

And so Mother dear, in the words of Paul and Timothy,
    "Rejoice in the Lord always;
    Again I will say, Rejoice.
    Let all men know your forbearance.
    The Lord is at hand.
    Have no anxiety about anything,
    But in everything by prayer and supplication
        with thanksgiving let your requests
        be made known to God.
    And the peace of God, which passes all
    Understanding, will keep your hearts and
    Minds in Christ Jesus.
    And the grace of the Lord Jesus Christ be with your
        spirit.
    Amen."

2 Finding Meaning

15 August 1980
Ottawa

With experienced eyes he measured—the lie and speed of
the translucent ice
—the position of the
opposing rocks
—the skip's broom.
With graceful stride his right arm swung
—the rock propelled in deadly course
—the take out was complete.
At *that* moment the coronary closed.
A blaze of pain—spinning rink.
blackness
Friends gathered 'round.
It was so fast.
Bill gone.
"It was as he would want it," someone said.
"He was doing what he loved."

I look across the room at you.
Mother, you look tired.
Your path a different one from Bill's
—it is by inches—
time is on our side!
or, it is against us?
Weakness,
cough,
fatigue,
a melting away,
perspiration

—but mainly the weakness.
"It is no joke," someone said.
We all agreed.
_____

So different these two paths.
The difference is time— for the one leaving
                         for those left behind.
Is it really a gift to go as Bill did? Without knowing.
Does an inching out of life hold only the promise of a
    prolongation of the pain?
No!
"Death destroys a man but the idea of death saves him."
                                             Forster was right.
To catch a glimpse of our own mortality in the prism of
    passing time
Is to see it all in fresh perspective.
The skip of heart beat when the thought sinks in
    "I will not pass this way again"
                         —sync!
    "This is the last time I will feel your gaze and touch"
                                   —sync!
    "Kind of grabs you when you realize you've just folded
    a fold-out tapestick for the very last time," said Ted.
                                   —sync!
Integration/Confrontation with reality/This is it./
                              World in a new focus.
But that was not all that Ted said. Not all.
          "I am *happier* for what I've been through."
Happier!
Happier?
Surely he was joking! But he wasn't you know. Dying, yet
    happier for what he'd been through. Not joking, you
    could tell; see it in his eyes.

But wherein lay his happiness?
The narrator said it all. He said it for Rosenthal, for Segal,
   For me, for you, Mother—for us all.
                    "When there's nothing left to hide
                    And no need to turn away
                    You can make a moment last a lifetime
                    Make a lifetime last a day."

Chip?
A shooting star!
He was magnificent. In body, mind and spirit.
Number one!
Living proof that while we are all born equal,
                    some are more equal than others!
Always the one voted
            "Most likely to"
            —then awarded the garlands when he "did."
Socially at ease. Athlete
                    Scholar
                    Executive.   Life—a trophy case
                                      Mountain following
                                          mountaintop.
Now, dying!
   —that marvelous body melting before the raging forces
      of the embryonal cell
   —the *very* differentiated overtaken by the undiffer-
      entiated
   —the *ultimate* giving way to the primitive.

You called us to your bedside, Chip.
To each you bid your private adieu.
Real class! Style—but not just that—Grace.
The grace that comes with growth.

———

Your love made my loss greater
   —not just "patient," but brother!
Through dry lips, and from your crumbling form,
your words struck an anvil chorus of contrast to the
    obvious.
   "This has been the best year of my life!"

You're kidding—
The best year? of *that* life? That was no average life, man.
                            Chip, superstar!

But amplified by grace those words needed no defense.
Their validity was clear.
Wonderment!
Frankl was / is right!
               From the stinking hell of Auschwitz
               came the first germ of insight.
               What driving force compels us?
                    lifts us?
                    lights our way?
               Not driven by thirst for power
                   by sexual urge
                   by quest for fame or fortune
               Man's search is for *meaning*.
That is it!
Chip, *that's* what it was!
Ted, that is why you were happier!

———

Let me find meaning Lord. When faced with finality
                  caught in the crucible!
"It is when we are down and experiencing a time of
adversity that we may be most able to open the doors of our

personalities and expose our needs."
No time for pretense.
Masks stripped away.
In the hard light of finality, so much that was treasured
        fades away—things,
                events—in the perspective of
                     this light they are
                          but dust.
Instead—
    time
    feelings
    relationships
    to relate to others.
To give—and in so doing to receive.
To become empty, by opening, so that we may be filled.
To recognize that only in dying can we find life
               —dying to ourselves
               —that we may be open to the other.

————

What tangled web of feelings   skills   uncertainties
                       perceptions   traits   perspectives
                             insecurities   inheritance
    shapes our course?
Am I free?
I do not understand. Why did I react?
                What fears lie hidden in some recess of
                my mind?
    You there!—Schweitzer—in your jungle home,
           "Driven collie-dog of a man," from
           what long-forgotten strands has
           your restless anguish risen?
    You there!—H. T. R.—where is your peace?

Where the satisfaction of knowing
the job has been well done?
Can we not be free?
Must we be bound to long forgotten circumstance?

_____

In these days we stand together before death
Awash in a sea of reality.
Strain
Tension
Communication block
Anger
Love and hate are one.
This maelstrom must lead to dissolution
or
union/integration.
Given this time, the potential that eluded Bill is ours.
With what tools do we re-examine these relationships?
Whence does reconciliation spring?

_____

Imprisoned in a Roman cell, his fertile mind was yet free.
It was on fire!
A burst of letters were sent out
—to Ephesus
—to Colossae
And yet another, to plead the case of one
convicted; now reformed.
He spoke to them,
He speaks to us.
We interrupt his train of thought
"Tell us sir—you there, pacing in your prison as you
dictate,
What can *you* tell us, in our quest for openness to other?
What then shall we do?"

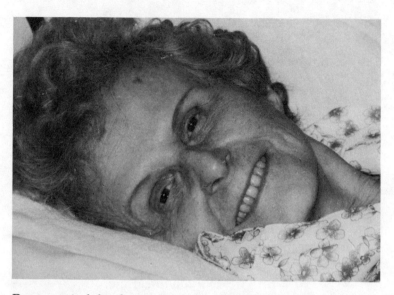

Preoccupied, he does not hear us, but a younger man steps
   forward to our aid. He lays a cautioning finger to his
   lips.
Tychicus hands us a copy of the texts he but
   recently delivered. His finger points.
We read:
   "I bow my knees before the Father,
   from whom every family in heaven and on earth is
   named, that according to the riches of his glory he may
   grant you to be strengthened with might through his
   Spirit in the inner man, and that Christ may dwell in
   your hearts through faith; that you, being rooted and
   grounded in love, may have power to comprehend
   with all the saints what is the breadth and length
   and height and depth, and to know the love of
   Christ which surpasses knowledge, that you
   may be filled with all the fulness of God.
   Now to him who by the power at work within us is

able to do far more abundantly than all that we ask
or think, to him be glory in the church and in
Christ Jesus to all generations, for ever and ever.
Amen."

_____

"Let all bitterness and wrath and anger and clamor and
slander be put away from you, with all malice, and be
kind to one another, tenderhearted, forgiving one
another, as God in Christ forgave you."

_____

"Put on then... compassion, kindness, lowliness,
meekness, and patience, forbearing one another and,
if one has a complaint against another, forgiving each
other; as the Lord has forgiven you, so you also must
forgive. And above all these put on love, which binds
everything together in perfect harmony. And let the
peace of Christ rule in your hearts."

_____

Suddenly the pacing stops.
The cell is quiet.
We are fixed by piercing eyes.
Train of thought broken.
Tychicus is silent.
Paul speaks: "So, you are concerned with meaning, love,
and reconciliation are you? From Ephesus
four years ago I sent another message to my
friends. Our brothers in evil Corinth were at
that time in great need of counsel. I believe
the centuries have not lessened *your* need for
insight in these matters, and so I tell you
as I told them—
'If I speak in the tongues of men and of angels,
But have not love,

I am a noisy gong or a clanging cymbal.
And if I have prophetic powers,
And understand all mysteries and all knowledge,
And if I have all faith,
So as to remove mountains,
But have not love,
I am nothing.
If I give away all I have,
And if I deliver my body to be burned,
But have not love,
I gain nothing.

Love is patient and kind;
Love is not jealous or boastful;
It is not arrogant or rude.
Love does not insist on its own way;
It is not irritable or resentful;
It does not rejoice at wrong,
But rejoices in the right.
Love bears all things,
Believes all things,
Hopes all things,
Endures all things.
Love never ends;
As for prophecies, they will pass away;
As for tongues, they will cease;
As for knowledge it will pass away.
For our knowledge is imperfect and our prophecy is
    imperfect;
But when the perfect comes, the imperfect will pass away.
When I was a child, I spoke like a child,
I thought like a child, I reasoned like a child;
When I became a man, I gave up childish ways.

For now we see in a mirror dimly, but then face to face.
Now I know in part; then I shall understand fully, even
    as I have been fully understood.
So faith, hope, love abide, these three; but the greatest
    of these is love.' "

———————

—Mother, do we ever learn to love?
                              to be open?
                              to accept   —the other?
                                            —ourselves?
              Can we ever learn who we are?
—Here we stand as a family.
      At least this way we have been stopped
              in our tracks; given time Bill did not have.
      The opportunity is ours
      to re-examine reality.
                      ourselves.
                      the other.
              First steps taken.
              Unfinished business started.

———————

Thank you.

3 Solace

16 August 1980
Ottawa

His hand-picked Levite court musicians knew not when
    he had composed it.
Some said it was as he lay waiting for the morning and his
    meeting with the Philistine.
Others whispered that it was inspired by knowledge of
    Saul's jealousy and the danger of his spear.
David, was it when leading your army into battle
That these words first came to you?
Or were they born years earlier, one lonely hillside night,
As your young eyes watched the restless sheep
And scanned the shadows for a foe?

Even in your day the solace in your words
Gave courage to the faithful heart.
You wrap us in your peace.

To us you left a double legacy: your song,
                  your Royal Lineage
                  —the one who followed you.
Shepherd, conqueror, king—you gave us
The good shepherd, conqueror of death, king of kings.

In this hour of need your song is on our lips.
The two of you are at our side.
United with you we recite:
    The Lord is my shepherd, I shall not want;
        he makes me lie down in green pastures.
    He leads me beside still waters;

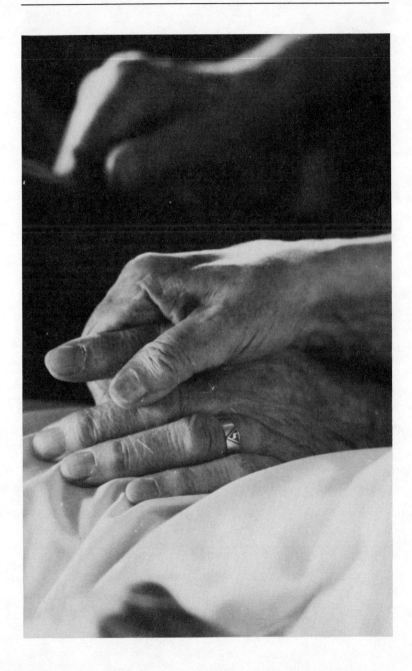

he restores my soul.
He leads me in paths of righteousness
    for his name's sake.
Even though I walk through the valley of the shadow
        of death,
    I fear no evil;
For thou art with me;
    thy rod and thy staff, they comfort me.
Thou preparest a table before me
    in the presence of my enemies;
Thou anointest my head with oil,
    my cup overflows.
Surely goodness and mercy shall follow me
    all the days of my life;
And I shall dwell in the house of the LORD for ever.

4 Priorities

17 August 1980
Ottawa

Priorities.
Someone said, "To know a man look at the list of his
    receipts."
Another day of decisions lies ahead,
Nothing major,
Just how I spend my time.

———

———

Working against a deadline
(It had been self-imposed)
To finish the planting before sundown,
The fresh energy and zest of dawn became
            fatigue, under mid-day's blistering sun,
            then hunger and exhaustion as the
            shadows lengthened.
Father will be pleased.
God, I'm tired! And I am starved!
I leave the fields behind
Walk toward the setting sun.
This road seems endless.
Dust
Sweat running in rivers
Feet burning
The aching in my back started hours ago.
Hunger stalks me like an eagle, wings beating over
    my body,
            talons buried in my gut.
            Its persistant shrill cry batters my ability
            to think.

Could eat an ox!
Oh for a flagon of wine!

————————

What's that smell?
Had I energy to run I would.
"By the heavens that smells good!"
God, I'm hungry!   —makes the cramps worse though.
Jacob's gruel! That's *one* thing he can do.
It isn't fair! While I toil dawn to dusk,
He rests and lazes in the tent.
"Let me eat some of that red pottage, brother. I am
    famished."
"First sell me your birthright."
"I am about to die."
"Swear to me first."
I did.
Would have perished otherwise.
Chunks of fresh bread dipped in lentil soup (smothered
    in butter)
A gourd of wine.
That feels better. Good to sit!
A *pox* on you Jacob, *and* the bloody birthright!

————————

————————

Wish I had been able to get away earlier.
Business was pressing.
Tied up all morning.
But if I hurry I will make it.
I hear he's leaving for Jerusalem today.
He's been in Judea several days now.
Must hurry.
Run!
There is something about him. He is brilliant. A real leader

—more than that though.
Yesterday the Pharisees tried to corner him.
I hear there have been healings.
The whole town is buzzing.
Say, that's strange, streets empty
                    —hardly anyone in the bazaar
          —bad for business.
                              —bet they're all out to hear him.
                        —there's never been anything like it!
                        —should have left earlier,
                    excuse me.
    Getting a little winded.
                              Must
                          get more
                          exercise.
There, I can hear them now.
Must be just over the next hill.
            Could probably see if it weren't for those trees.
    " 'Scuse me."
            "You *there*. Watch out!"
                    "Sorry!"
Look at that crowd!
          (I'll never get through)
They're breaking up.
Can't catch my breath.

Children.
Wonder what all those children are doing.

There he is!
That face!
That mother certainly looks happy. He's handing the child
    back to her.

He's coming this way! " 'Scuse me."
      "Sorry."
          (thank you)
Face to face.
Those eyes!
     Never have I seen eyes like that.
"Good Teacher, what shall I do to inherit eternal life?"
"Why do you call me Good? No one is good but God alone.
   You know the commandments. Do not commit adultery,
   do not steal, do not bear false witness, honor your
     father and mother."
"All these I have observed from my youth."
"One thing you still lack. Sell all you have and distribute
   to the poor,
   And you will have treasure in heaven; and come, follow
     me."
Those eyes. He sees through my very soul.
He knows me.
So close.
Those eyes. Gentle. Warm. Loving.
Bond of understanding between us.
We could accomplish much together.
Sell all I have?
Sell *all*?
How could I? They all depend on me.
Sell all? Give to the poor? That makes no sense.
     I am giving to them now.
How many programs for the poor I have started!
Sell all? Unable would I then be to do all that I
   now do.
Sell all? Who would support the synagogue?
Just yesterday they came to me about the need for
     a new roof for the temple.

Sell all? He can't be serious! I would be naked.
                                    stripped.
                                    shorn.

_____

"Wait.
Don't go.
What did you say?   Did you hear that sir?
                     What was that about a camel
                     entering the city gate?"
Can't hear
     —people in the way.
"Wait!"
   He's gone.
     Finished.

_____

Maude, Maude, I'm sorry.
So many things I wish I'd done.
I was always in the O.R. by eight you know
And I had to see patients in the evenings, sometimes
                                    in three
                                    hospitals.
So many people needed me.
The children grew up. I wasn't there.
So much I have missed. Oh Maude!

_____

_____

Hi. . . . That you dear? . . . Sorry I am late. . . .
Listen, I am swamped.
Grant application has to be done tonight
And there are two consults yet to do.
Gotta go.
They're waiting for me for a meeting.

... Go ahead without me.... Maybe someone else
   can use my ticket.
... Kids O.K.?... Not again!
Well listen, I gotta go. Tell me about it later....
... Oh, ya....Well I'll be asleep when you get in....
I'm bushed....
Tell me tomorrow.
Bye!

———

———

They're always bugging me. Cut the grass!
                                 Walk the dog!
                                 Study!
Need a smoke! Turn on some music.
Damn! I can't! Already late for the jam.
Need new strings.
Blew the amp yesterday.
Wonder how the new song will sound.
There she goes again!
Always yellin'!
I'll just slip out the front door.
They'll never miss me.
Need a smoke.

———

———

Well, Lord, another night.
It's been another day of decisions
Nothing major
Just how I spend my time.

5 Freedom

19 August 1980
The Place

I closed my eyes and saw a form
A shapeless angled mass
Brownish
Heavy
Lying still upon the cliff.
Self.
And as I watched I opened
And my inner self escaped.
A butterfly
Rising happily on lightly beating wings
    to freedom
        peace.
But alas, 'twas but a dream within a dream.
In the confines of this mass I must remain.
Why, Mother?

————

————

Dust of the street corner, she is of no great worth.
Bent by unseen burdens;
Gripped these eighteen years by a spirit of infirmity,
She is well known within the town.
You've seen her many times beside the well.
I'm sure you know her.
—(At last, it is my turn!)
—(Here sister, hold this while I draw my water.)
Well, yesterday she came to the synagogue.
There was a crowd.
There always is, you know, when the Nazarene's about.

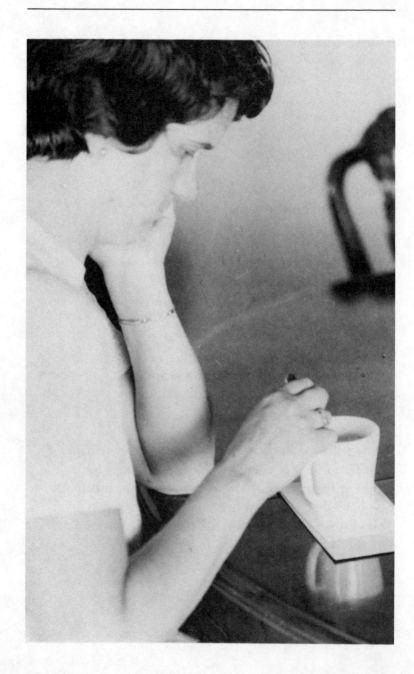

He taught.
Marvelous voice he has.
And his *eyes*!
Well, anyway, things were doing fine when suddenly he
    stopped.
Right in the middle of the lesson!
And he spoke to *her*!
And her a *woman*, and all!

Would you believe it?

Right in the synagogue!
Frankly, I was shocked!
"Woman, you are freed from your infirmity," he said.
And immediately she was made straight.
Right as rain!
Well! You should have heard the ruckus!
She began carrying on and praising God.
But the ruler of the synogogue, he set them straight.
—(Just one minute sister.)
—(I've another jug to fill.)
—(You'll get your turn. Be patient girl.)
He chastized the Nazarene.
No need to desecrate the sabbath, don't you know.
Each week there are six other days to heal.
But the teacher, he spoke up!
He called them hypocrites!
Sister, it was tense!
I tell you, you could fairly feel the fire in the air!
His eyes, they blazed.
His voice rang out.
Called her a daughter of Abraham, he did,
And asked, was she not worth as much

As the ox and ass they harness up
To water on each sabbath morn.
And they had no answer for him.
Once more the shouts of praise and joy went up.
I tell you sister it was a memorable day!
You should have been there!
The old crone is like new!
(Here sister, help me place that jug upon my
    other shoulder...)
Farewell!... until tomorrow then.

Where shall we turn to be made whole?
Where lies the healing that we seek?
I labor Lord
And heavy laden am.
Can I find my rest
    in
        you?

6 Integrating

19 August 1980
The Place

Can't sleep.
I'm restless, Mother.
It is still dark.
I dress
And on the dock I watch the morning mists take form
   and rise.
In the gathering light
           silence
               breathless air
                   hills suspend.
Far off, a loon cries.
A new day.

———

Will this one be your last, Mother?
Is that why those fingers grip my heart?
How many more?
I am afraid
       —for you!
            —for me?
                 —for both of us?

———

We are in a play. We all have parts. And we all rely on you.
Producer, director, a member of the cast.
Each task you carry off with great panache.
This week it is a comedy.
—A pathetic little piece
Of people caught up in their needs
Unable to hear each other's lines.

Each actor has a fantasy
And in attempting to make it real—destroys the very
    thing he would create.
It's really very comical!
While the writing's mediocre, the acting is refined.
You see, each actor has been playing the same part
    for many years!

Mists rising
Boats drifting
Silence.
Seeing as how it's just a play,
It's hard to realize it's real!
That oil slick, drifting there upon the water
    —that's real enough.
Reality!
    You are always just an illusion away.
    Always just around the corner.
    Today you are all too ready to take off your mask.
    I like to think I seek you.
    Today I'm not so sure.
    Rather play act.
    Rather have Mother well.

Dying
The finality crushes.
Adam, you really screwed it up.
Not that it's so bad here east of Eden
But were we really meant to die?

Father be with her.
Protect her.
To your loving arms I commit her.

Can see distinctly now.
Needles of the great white pines
Etched starkly against the brightening sky.

At the very end, Father, will it be difficult?
Some who walk with you, Lord, find it so.
Judy did.
Nouwen's mother.
Mother, will you?

"Eli, Eli, lama sabach-thani?"
Like thunder, the words rang out in the darkness.
For three hours it had been black
An eerie stillness save for the women weeping.
And the pounding of my heart.
"Here I'll give you some of this vinegar mixture
To take away the thirst."
              "Wait, let us see whether
              Elijah will save him."
His face!—can you see it?
Blood.
Sweat.
But that expression!
Do you remember how he used to look
When he was teaching?
Like a man on fire with peace!
Such certainty!
Such strength!
Did you see his face just now?
Empty agony.
My God, did you see it?
His legs were twitching, his chest heaving,

Blood and sweat in rivers flow
But it is that face that evermore will haunt me.
Did you see it?
Shattered.
Broken
In despair
I have seen hell!

_____

Tasha stretches
Rolls over in the sand
Yawns.
A mosquito's whine cuts the silence.
Her tail beats gently as she sees me.

_____

In darkness Mary Magdalene went slowly to the tomb.
Each halting step echoed back her grief.
She could at first see dimly.
Surely, she must be wrong.
She checked the spot.
                And terror gripped her.
                    It was *empty*.
Empty!
Gaping!
Stone rolled away. His body gone.
Wild drumming terror.... "I must get Peter."
                —her feet flew—
He was with John.
Back to the tomb they ran
                    nightmare or reality?
                    pounding fear!
                    all worlds in disarray.
                    fragmentation.
Empty.

John saw its void and knelt. Despair.
Peter charged on past him without pause. Frantic!
The clothes lay folded.
Mary followed. Stumbling—
She looked and saw in dazzling light two figures
    sitting in the crypt.
"Woman why are you weeping?"
In agony, she noted not the splendor of their form.
"Because they have taken away my lord, and I do not
    know where they have laid him."
Hot tears.
Burning breathlessness.
She turned.
There in the shadows of a new dawn a figure stood.
"Woman why are you weeping? Whom do you seek?"
Must be the gardener. She choked a sob.
"Sir if you have carried him away, tell me where you
    have laid him and I will take him away."

One word in response.
A single word came singing through fresh morning air.
Igniting every fiber of her being.
Setting her soul ablaze.
Bursting in her with new light and life.
"Mary."
She turned.
She saw him clearly now.
Stop Time.
All eternity summed up in that face.
          Those eyes
          That smile
"Rabboni!"

———————

Sleeping figures stir.
A fish jumps.
Mists clear.
Day dawns.
A bird sings.

———————

But in fact Christ has been raised from the dead,
The first fruits of those who have fallen asleep.
For as by a man came death,
By a man has come also the resurrection of the dead.
For as in Adam all die,
So also in Christ shall all be made alive.
What is sown is perishable,
What is raised is imperishable.
It is sown in dishonor,
It is raised in glory.
It is sown in weakness,
It is raised in power.
It is sown a physical body,

It is raised a spiritual body.
If there is a physical body, there is also a spiritual body.
Thus it is written, "The first man became a living being";
The last Adam became a life-giving spirit.
But it is not the spiritual which is first but the physical,
And then the spiritual.
The first man was from earth, a man of dust;
The second man is from heaven.
As was the man of dust, so are those who are of heaven.
Just as we have borne the image of the man of dust,
We shall also bear the image of the man of heaven.
I tell you this, brethren:
Flesh and blood cannot inherit the kingdom of God,
Nor does the perishable inherit the imperishable.
Lo! I tell you a mystery.
We shall not all sleep, but we shall all be changed,
In a moment, in the twinkling of an eye, at the last trumpet.
For the trumpet shall sound,
And the dead will be raised imperishable,
And we shall be changed.
For this perishable nature must put on the imperishable.
And this mortal nature must put on immortality.
When the perishable puts on the imperishable,
And the mortal puts on immortality,
Then shall come to pass the saying that is written:
    "Death is swallowed up in victory"
    "O death, where is thy victory?"
    "O death, where is thy sting?"

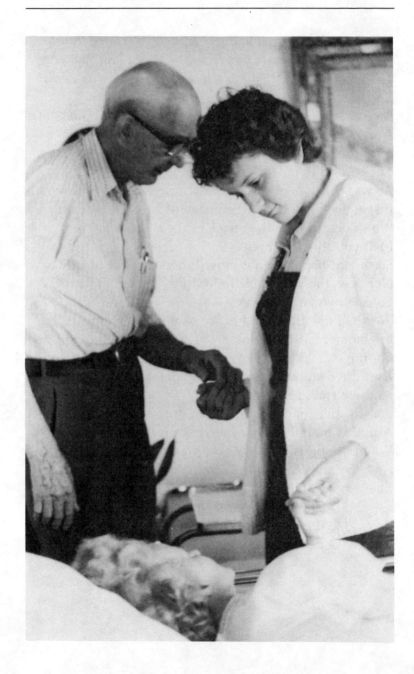

7 Final Encounters

20 August 1980
The Place

Two doves fluttered in the cage that dangled from
    his hand.
Testimony to their humble means.
They walked in silence, sharing a deep joy,
In anticipation of the cleansing act.
The forty days,
Since first he filled their lives with light,
Seemed but a breath.
—So much; so short a time!
From cattle stall to history's center stage!
Who could comprehend?
Who but those who, armed with faith,
Could see with clearer sight—a mother
                        —an old man.

_____

The couple reached the temple.
In the east gate of the court the priest waited.
All was in readiness.
The husband passed the cage to his left hand and took
    her arm.
She smiled at his touch.
The baby seemed to sleep.

_____

Suddenly,
The court was filled with light.
Rich golden hues of the setting sun.
The old man's eyes were on them.
And for a timeless instant

They all stood, bathed in brilliance.
Their eyes met.

———————

Destined synchrony of timing,
He had entered with them but by another door.
A voice had spoken.
A promise had been made.
In response, propelled by faith, he came.
Four centuries of silence had been broken.
And in his heart he knew he'd not see death
'Til he had seen the Christ.

———————

In faith he saw the infant's face.
In faith his aged form advanced.
In faith he reached and took the child.

With cosmic understanding, she no resistance made.
    Stop Time
            moment of destiny
                completion
                    inner peace.

———————

That bearded head turned heavenward.
He'd seen the circle closed.
Nation's and man's, both longings were fulfilled.
He spoke,
    "Lord, now lettest thou thy servant depart in peace,
    According to thy word;
    For mine eyes have seen thy salvation
    Which thou hast prepared
    In the presence of all peoples,
    A light for revelation to the Gentiles,
    And for glory to thy people Israel."

How many Simeons, Lord,
Have been nurtured by your gaze? How many have found
Darkness vanquished in your light, have been
Sustained by you in their final days?
How many Lord
Have known your touch
Since first your eyes looked up
And
Saw that aged face?

"Please give her a message," the caller said.
"Tell her Miss Brown cannot come today.
But in our place we send a gift.
Give her Isaiah 30:15!"
Miss Vallor listened with great intent.
With trace of smile she quietly explained
"My friend Miss Brown is filled with grace.
I mark her words with utmost care.
Fifty years are gone
Since first she led me in his path.
The thought that comes from her today
Must be reflected on."
    —"In quietness and confidence
      Shall be your strength."

I took her hand.
She settled in a drifting sleep.
Minutes passed. I rose to go.
In radiance, she smiled and looked into my eyes.
"It was wonderful," she said.

"Just now, I was with Jesus.
He was sitting on a hill.
Small children were around him.
There were flowers everywhere."
Her lips were dry.
Her limbs were cold
But her eyes, they softly shone
With a sparkling inner light.
Once more she slept.
Again I stirred to leave. Her eyes opened.
"This time I saw him fishing with his men.
They were on the sea
          —And I was there."

The following days were filled with peace.
Then frail life ebbed away.
Miss Vallor died.
A life spent walking by your side.

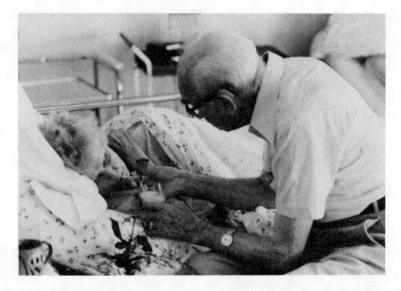

What of her life?
Grey?
Restricted?
Worn around the edges?
Most would say it had been difficult.
Its pages crossed with cares.
Few frills had marked the chapters of its passing.
No earthly trumpets sounded her dying hour.
It was not mentioned in the *Times*!
Yet by that bed, through her, I looked into your eyes.
I saw her take your hand.
Sustained—she looked at death—but could see only you.

As her eyes closed, I heard you say,
"As you did it to one of the least of these my brethren,
You did it to me."
Thus in that hospice ward,
As in that temple long ago,
You came to both of us.
And we with Simeon stood
In joining the vast company,
Meeting you in death.

8 Where's It At?

22 August 1980
The Place

What's it all about?
The big goal.
Where's it at?
When the chips are down what makes you run?

The answers were unhesitating.
"To make it to the top: to be the very best!"
"To be liked, sir."
"To be desired. Why, I'll be playmate of the year!"
"To promote our cause. It's growing you know.
There are more of us each year"
"peace"
"ecology"
"women's movement"
"natural childbirth"
"ban the hunt"
"I've never thought about it."
"To have no goals at all."
"To win more souls for Christ, my friend."
"Like to have the ultimate turn on, man! To be stoned
out of my mind!"
"To understand myself. I seek freedom and inner
peace."
"To have power."
"To tell it like it is, baby!"
"To cleanse myself of all impurity."
"To climb that mountain."
"Just to make it through today."

"I'm not sure. Why do you ask?"
"To be elected."
"To be published."
"To own my own business."
"No comment."
"To discover."
"To have my works on display."
"Why, to double our sales in the eastern provinces."
"To own a bigger. . . ."
"To be without hunger."
"To travel."
"To shoot down one more plane."
"To have relief from pain."
"To spend time with my kids."
"To have her love me."
"To be rid of this infirmity."
"To pass the exams."
"To lose that fear."
"To be recognized."
"To drive a Porsche."
"To see my congregation grow."
"To win equality for our race."
"To win the championship / set a new record."
"To kill!"
"To enjoy myself."
"To fall in love again."
"To promote a sell-out match."
"To cut our losses."
"To make love perfectly."
"To conceal what I really am."
"To write a song like that again."
"To see an end to *their* political system."
"To be taller."

"smaller"
"prettier"
"of a different race."
"To drive the enemy out."
"To be respected."
"To be responsive."
"To catch the perfect wave."
And you sir, what about you?
"To feed the hungry, give drink to the thirsty,
to welcome the stranger, clothe the naked,
visit the sick and imprisoned."
You're kidding!

Enter by the narrow gate;
For the gate is wide and the way is easy,
That leads to destruction,
And those who enter by it are many.
For the gate is narrow and the way is hard,
That leads to life,
And those who find it are few.

9 Promises Kept

22 August 1980
The Place

Father we give thanks
—for Jesus
—for his teachings and presence with us.
Open our ears Lord to all that you would have us hear.
Fire us with a new understanding of the Scriptures and
their meaning for us in this time of need.
Open our hearts to receive your Spirit.

You proclaim release to the captives, Lord.
—Father, we are enslaved in so many ways!
Captive to our present circumstance
—our lack of understanding
—our failure to accept ourselves.
We are captive to our fears and doubts.
—Release us, Lord, from these bonds.
Help us to comprehend that your offer is meant
for us!
Here and now!
Lord, you proclaim recovery of sight to the blind.
—Father, we are only able to see our own needs
at this time. We are blind to anything good in all
this. We can see no reason for what is happening.
Often we are even blind to your presence Lord.
—We pray for clearer vision.
—Open our eyes that we may see your presence in
today.
Lord, you promise liberty to the oppressed.
—Today we are under the gun.

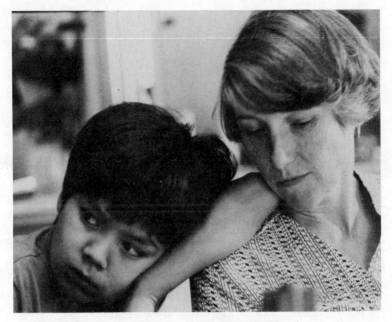

Chained. In danger of being crushed.
—We are in need of the liberty that only
you can give.
—Abide in us Lord, and we in you. Fill us with
your peace that passes all understanding, that
we may more perfectly follow you—and make it
through today.

Jesus, you speak of good news.
What is the good news for us today?
—Surely it is that you died for us
and that in dying you have conquered death.
—That you are with us here and now.
—In this room
—A suffering God.
Sharing in our time of need.
We are not alone!

10 On Healing

24 August 1980
The Place

Jairus, ruler in the synagogue,
His daughter dying, then reported dead.
"Do not fear; only believe, and she shall be well," you said.

You came down from the mountain
And the leper spoke in faith,
"Lord, if you will, you can make me clean."
"I will; be clean" was your reply.

Those healings in Judea long ago were signs,
A demonstration of your power and love.
Not a cure-all, a celestial reward
When the rabbit's foot called faith is rubbed.
Not a measure of faith,
But an explosion of your being in history,
Catalyzed by faith.
Your intervention in our daily lives
Is my experience.
Usually you work within your law,
But that is not the point.
The explanation does not the miracle define.
How myopic is the view that sees you only in those things
    that aren't explained!
Are penicillin and sunsets lesser miracles
Because we understand them?
When we more fully understand the activated lymphocyte
And the impact of the psyche on disease,

Will regression of pathology be lessened in our eyes?
The jaundiced eye of modern man has self-sufficiency
     enough
To block the vision of you standing by our side.
When we fail to see your hand in all that touches us,
We use the eyes that failed to see your covenants with man.
Those in the arc,
The rainbow hues,
And finally the cross.
Funny thing about life! It must be seen through opened
     eyes
To see the essence of reality
          the font of *all* reality
               —standing by our side.

_____

_____

Joe glowed.
So did his wife—but like a bowstring,
          taut,
               forced joy,
                    pressurized "peace."
They were followers of your word.
"Ask, and it will be given you. . . .
For everyone who asks receives."
To Kathryn Kuhlman they had gone.
The response of his protruding eye was indeed
     miraculous.
No less so, caused as it was by radiotherapy.
But recent therapy was forgotten in a euphoria of belief!
And now catch 22!
All therapy must be stopped.
For how could one need ancillary aids
Once touched by your healing hand?

To even suspect further ills was to doubt your power.
"I *do* believe! I must be cured! To doubt will spell my
    doom!"
Trapped by faith!
    By faith?
Something wrong there, Joe!

In truth the tragedy was compounded.
For in that forced charade, the real miracle was missed.
Your presence with him, this man of faith ignored.
By looking only where *he* sought you
Joe closed to your availability.

To see the miracle we must open,
Not close in desperate fear.

The days that followed were filled with hollow joy
The fantasy was fed by energy and time Joe could ill afford.

> Communication blocked
> True feelings were repressed
> Crisis of anxiety
> Faith misunderstood
> World gone awry

Fine beads of perspiration.
Though the evening was warm, your limbs were cold
Heart pounding
            leaden weight
                all in vain?
                    blackness!
You took with you Peter, James and John.
How often they had bantered, marveled at your word.

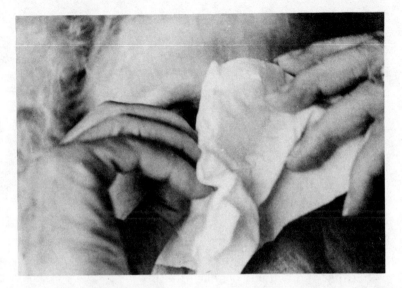

This time lost in silence.
Their eyes heavy, yours were deeply troubled.
Their minds dulled for sleep, yours racing.
"My soul is very sorrowful, even unto death;
Remain here, and watch a while with me. . . .
Pray that you may not give in to temptation."

You went on alone.
The soft lights of the city far below seemed distant
In that garden of despair.
To your knees you fell.
"My Father, if it be possible, let this cup pass from me;
Nevertheless not as I will, but as thou wilt."
Your disciples slept.
"My Father, if this cannot pass unless I drink it,
Thy will be done."
His answer?
Torches coming toward you up the hill.

A whirling sequence ending in the cross.

_____

_____

In the hospital bed I lay
Numbed with overwhelming recognition of reality.
Malignant!
My garden scene was played out in the Ross.
"If you are with me here Lord, now is the hour to speak!
Let's have it *now*: a sign, a word from you!"
Like yours, my prayer in earnest given.
The Bible opened at the Psalms.
116, I had not read before.
　"I love the LORD, because he has heard
　　My voice and my supplications.
　Because he inclined his ear to me,
　　Therefore I will call on him as long as I live.
　The snares of death encompassed me;
　　The pangs of Sheol laid hold on me,
　　I suffered distress and anguish.
　Then I called on the name of the LORD:
　　'O LORD, I beseech thee, save my life!'

_____

　Gracious is the LORD, and righteous;
　　Our God is merciful.
　The LORD preserves the simple;
　　When I was brought low, he saved me.
　Return, O my soul, to your rest;
　　For the LORD has dealt bountifully with you.

_____

　For thou hast delivered my soul from death,
　　My eyes from tears,
　　My feet from stumbling;
　I walk before the LORD

In the land of the living.
I kept my faith, even when I said,
    'I am greatly afflicted';
I said in my consternation,
    'Men are all a vain hope.'

What shall I render to the LORD
    For all his bounty to me.
I will lift up the cup of salvation
    And call on the name of the LORD,
I will pay my vows to the LORD
    In the presence of all his people.
Precious in the sight of the LORD
    Is the death of his saints.
O LORD, I am thy servant;
    I am thy servant, the son of thy handmaid.
    Thou hast loosed my bonds.
I will offer to thee the sacrifice of thanksgiving
    And call on the name of the LORD.
I will pay my vows to the LORD
    In the presence of all his people,
In the courts of the house of the LORD,
    In your midst, O Jerusalem.
Praise the LORD!''

My heart leapt.
I was wrapped in your peace.

Two prayers in earnest
Mine answered, yours ignored?
"Sounds unlikely," as the saying goes.
For God was surely in that garden as your disciples slept.
Where then, in that suffering, did your Father act?

Where was his omnipotence?

———

The lesson from the garden is that God is with us in
    our pain.
He is in the *heart* of suffering, his the greater load.
A suffering deity, he bears our every scar.
The omnipotence of our Father
Is not expressed
Through the banishing of our ills
But in their ultimate defeat
Through his gift to us
Of his all-sufficient grace.

———

The last of human freedoms,
Frankl said,
Is not a freedom from all pain
But the freedom left to choose
Our response in the given circumstance.
And as we make the choice
We are shored by your presence at our side.
Supported!—not alone!
Cradled in your nail-pierced hands.

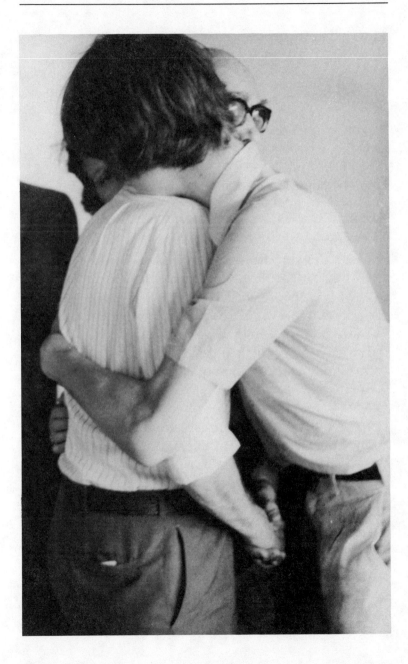

11 On Transience

30 August 1980
300 Driveway, Ottawa

Precious hours of sharing.
Minutes magnified.
I look into your eyes
And recognize the meaning of these moments.

A cloud,
    A rainbow,
        Dew on the morning grass,
           The flowers that make us
             pause at their perfection.
—These things were *meant* to be transient!
These things we hold in passage.
The evanescence of their beauty heightens our response.
But surely *this* form cannot be passing from me!
Surely this life that gave me life cannot depart!

To hold each other in gazes that mutually recognize
The ephemeral nature of this path
Is to share in the pain and meaning of all life.
To share in our anticipated grief,
To minister as I've been ministered to,
To share the recognition that we are standing
On the threshold of the stars,
And to bid you farewell—but for a while,
These are the priceless balms that heal
    my
        opening
           wounds.

———

Irregular heartbeat pounding on your ribs.
Moments of confusion.
> "I didn't know that little bell could
>   sound like that."
Increased need for sleep.

———

Don't go, friend.
Comrade.
We will miss you, Mother.

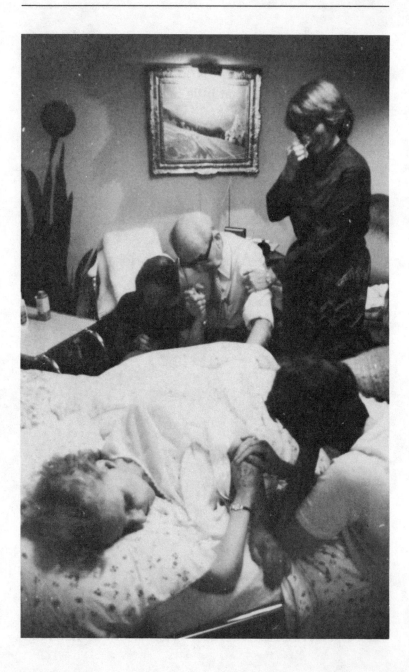

12 Home Care

30-31 August 1980
Ottawa

Outside,
    Thunder rolling,
    Erratic tongues of lightning split the firmament.
    Sheets of rain
    Driven by the fury of the wind.
Inside,
    The calm of order and good care,
    Sips of water,
    Clean sheets.
    The soft bells
    Bringing with their vision of peace and misty slopes
        the message, "It is all right."
    Absence of troubling symptoms save for the tide
    Of weakness—continually rising.
    Watching,
        waiting,
            listening,
                sharing in hushed tones.
Within,
    peace ringed round by heaviness.
Nature convulses about us
And at the epicenter of this storm
Frail life ebbs.
The power of God and the weakness of man contrasted.
We stand in awe of both.
Give me today, Lord,
The mind and heart to rejoice in thy creations!

Make a joyful noise to the LORD, all the lands!
Serve the LORD with gladness!
Come into his presence with singing!
Know that the LORD is God!
It is he that made us, and we are his;
We are his people, and the sheep of his pasture.
Enter his gates with thanksgiving,
And his courts with praise!
Give thanks to him, bless his name!
For the LORD is good;
His steadfast love endures for ever,
And his faithfulness to all generations.

Home care?
Isolated from the swirling storm
Opening—to you, Lord.
            —to each other.
Finding in these tempering days
Your gentle touch.

The bed is where the table was,
But nothing seems misplaced.
Life's cycles surround her
      —infant with a rash
      —the gifts of grandchild hands
      —bearded youth
      —the furnishings and mementos of a lifetime
      —sons in paunchy middle years
      —watching, caring eyes
      —laughter and sharing
      —aged spouse.
Below us the winding waterway and trees—
A gull soars.

Could that be Jonathan Livingston?
She rises off her pillow to watch that arcing flight.
"Look!"
Flowers on the balcony stir.

—————

The ever-present music casts its tranquil spell,
Soft bells, Joe Wise, Susan's sounds for relaxation.
And then by choice we share a gift.
As shadows lengthen we enter
The world of Joan Sutherland.
Spirits transported.
Your gifts surround us Lord
  Water shimmering with a thousand reflections
  From street lights and the passing cars
  —a muted symphony of dancing light.
  Joan's voice easily ripples in matching synchrony—
  Love experienced.
In giving we receive.
So many givers.
So many receivers.
So many gifts.
Home care?
It is the gift of time and space.
A space for integration of this dread reality.
To hold her hand,
To cool her brow with unexpected cloth and see
    her joy,
To minister, as we have received,
To taste her pleasure at the taste of water,
To share in this experience.

—————

—————

Thank you, Lord.

———
———

Night passes into day.
Misty morning, blurring the edges of
The water-color world below in softness.
   I lift up my eyes to the hills.
   From whence does my help come?
   My help comes from the LORD,
   Who made heaven and earth.
   He will not let your foot be moved,
   He who keeps you will not slumber.
   Behold, he who keeps Israel
   Will neither slumber nor sleep.
   The LORD is your keeper;
   The LORD is your shade
   On your right hand.
   The sun shall not smite you by day,
   Nor the moon by night.
   The LORD will keep you from all evil;
   He will keep your life.
   The LORD will keep
   Your going out and your coming in
   From this time forth and for evermore.

Those flowers say it all.
Transient magnificence, they are
Symbols of your love with us.
Petunias pruned, their growth to nurture.
You prune us too Lord.
May we, even in small measure, so reflect your love,
     Bless the LORD, O my soul;
     And all that is within me,
     Bless his holy name!

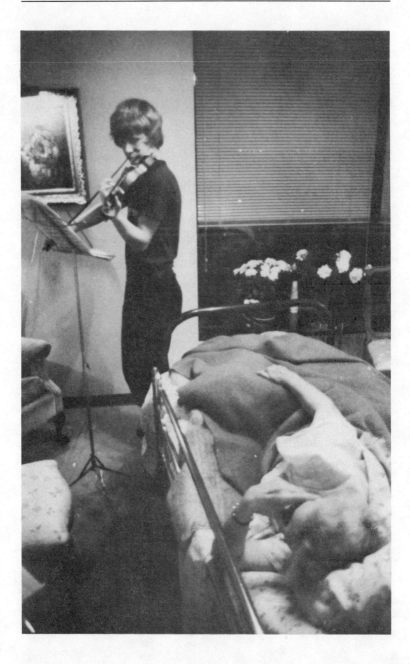

As for man, his days are like grass;
He flourishes like a flower of the field;
For the wind passes over it, and it is gone,
And its place knows it no more.
But the steadfast love of the LORD is
From everlasting to everlasting
Upon those who fear him,
And his righteousness to children's children,
To those who keep his covenant
And remember to do his commandments.
The LORD has established his throne in the heavens,
And his kingdom rules over all.

We part tonight.
Briefly?
When shall I see your face again?
To his loving hands I commit you, dear one.
  O give thanks unto the LORD; for he is good:
    For his mercy endureth for ever.
  O give thanks unto the God of gods:
    For his mercy endureth for ever.
    God is our refuge and strength,
      A very present help in
        Trouble.

Home care?
The gift of time and space
Integration on the edge of eternity.

13 Prayer

5 September 1980
Ottawa

Family prayer. We take our turn.
The five of us from so long ago
Gathered
In our incompleteness.
A buzzer heralds the arrival
Of the night nurse
Eight floors below.

Her lips open, and in a whisper
She gives voice to our hearts' plea.
    "Bless the one who stands at the door.
    Bless her doubly.
    Bless us all.
        In Christ's name.
        Amen."

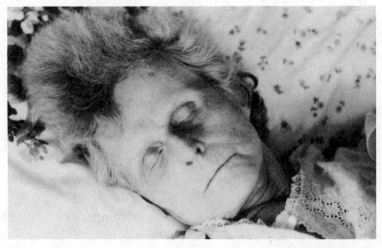

14 For Everything a Season

6 September 1980
Ottawa

Let me tell you all about tidal waves.
I have analyzed, studied,
Monitored, lectured, photographed and reported on them.
　　　　How different
　　　　To be
　　　　Engulfed
　　　　By one!

———

———

Inspired transmitter of eternal truth
Years had passed since he had penned his song,
Since proverbs had been written.
Now in old age he lived his penitence.
He saw the vanity of earthly goals through opened eyes.
Solomon—preacher, king, servant of the Lord—
Spoke to all whose ears were open to the word.
　For everything there is a season,
　And a time for every matter under heaven:
　A time to be born, and a time to die;
　A time to plant, and a time to pluck up what is planted;
　A time to kill, and a time to heal;
　A time to break down, and a time to build up;
　A time to weep, and a time to laugh;
　A time to mourn, and a time to dance;
　A time to cast away stones, and a time to gather
　　stones together;
　A time to embrace, and a time to refrain from
　　embracing;

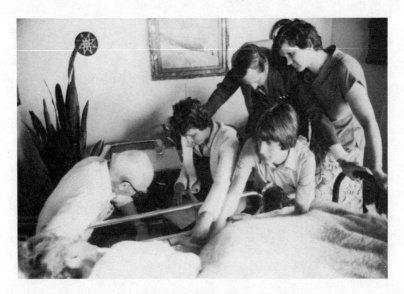

A time to seek, and a time to lose;
A time to keep, and a time to cast away;
A time to rend, and a time to sew;
A time to keep silence, and a time to speak;
A time to love, and a time to hate;
A time for war, and a time for peace.

———

Beams of sunlight casting patterned shadows
Across the floor beneath her bed.
Muffled voices.
She sleeps.
  Suspended moments
  Outside of time.
  Closing.

———

One block away, the children!
First day of classes!
Strange newness fills the air.

Brownian motion of young lives
In agitated joy.
Aripple with the pulse of life
Tumbling, balancing, standing, sitting, striding,
    jostling, looking, laughing.
But mostly, opening.

A time for everything?
No one took the pulse of time like him.
Enigma incarnate—all man; all God.
Defining contradiction, he was without contradiction.
For everything he saw a season.

Tempo picking up.
Intensity.
Destiny apprehended in each passing moment.
    Apprehension.
        Pulses quickening.
The thunderous welcome of the day before still
Echoed in their ears.
They'd spent the night in Bethany.
Their sleep had been disturbed by their uncertainty.
His by certainty.
They watched him as he walked.
He looked drawn, but they did not ask
If he had spent the starlit hours
Communing with his Father.
His pace was faster than their custom,
Charged with meaning in each step.
He was hungry.
No one spoke.
Silhouetted against the sky
The fig tree stood alone.

Surrealistic.
In leaf.
His eyes searched its fruitless branches.
Barren!
Omen!   *Stop Time.*
Crossroads of perception
    —man's hunger
    —God's judgment.
Flash of insight.
He saw the moral obstacles that would block
The path of those who would seek his kingdom.
"May no one ever eat fruit from you again."
Miraculous curse.
A warning for all time
That no stumbling block should stand
Before a confiding faith in God.
Withered to its roots!
They, in wonderment, looked on.
In awe they questioned him, and he replied.
"Have faith in God.
Truly I say to you,
Whatever you ask in prayer,
Believe that you have received it, and it will be yours."

Engulfed by his tidal wave
He saw in broader terms.
We see but dimly!
Our view is circumscribed.
Your eyes are wide, Mother. Be not afraid.
    "Why do you just let me die?
    Why don't you do something?
    I've been dying for so long."
    "O Maude."

"O Mother."
"It is not in our hands.
You know our love.
In God's hands you rest.
We are doing all we can."
Impotence!
   Are we?
      Has all been done?

_____

_____

"Sir, we wish to see Jesus," they had said.
Men from the west,
Like the wise men of the east who marked his birth.
Completing a circle.
At both ends of that brief trajectory, men came to him
And still they do.
With full heart, he looked into their trusting eyes.
Andrew and Philip,
Bearers of the Greek request to *see* him.
They know not what they ask, he thought.
He looked at them,
            but saw the cross.
He answered not their petition for an interview.
Lost in thought,
Consumed in scenes of triumph out of agony,
He spoke.
   "The hour has come for the Son of man to be glorified.
   Truly, truly, I say to you,
   Unless a grain of wheat falls into the earth and dies,
   It remains alone;
   But if it dies, it bears much fruit.
   He who loves his life loses it,
   And he who hates his life in this world will keep it

for eternal life.
If any one serves me, he must follow me;
And where I am, there shall my servant be also;
If any one serves me, the Father will honor him.
Now is my soul troubled.
And what shall I say?
'Father, save me from this hour'?
No,
For this purpose I have come to this hour.
Father,
Glorify thy name."
Then a voice came from heaven,
  "I have glorified it, and shall again."
"What was that?" they asked.
"Thunder?"
"An angel's call?"
It was his tidal wave—as he perceived it.
      And through him we begin
          to perceive.

15 Enemy Unmasked

7 September 1980
Ottawa

Vainly we strive to make the picture balance.
There must be reason, beauty, grace.
There must be meaning here.
Perhaps a hallelujah chorus.
            We miss the point!
The agony of the cross too often forgotten.

Death is not romantic.
Death *is* the enemy! Phyllis, you were right.
I saw him here today
    —without disguise.
    His mask of gentleness had slipped
    But he
    No longer cared.
She is moaning.
Weakness imprisons.
Not pain, but the restlessness of rupturing life.
Anguish, Cicely called it.
Anguish.

Translucent skin.
A spark gone out somewhere—
            From her eye
                    her spirit
Whole body pulsing
Quivering in futile defiance of the
Abyss that is too near.
Sunken features that I love

Form misshapen
No longer reaching out to us
No longer other centered.
Decathexis
A shrinking of her world
        to self
                to suffering
                        to death.
This is the *work* of dying.

Labor

Birth pangs of another life.

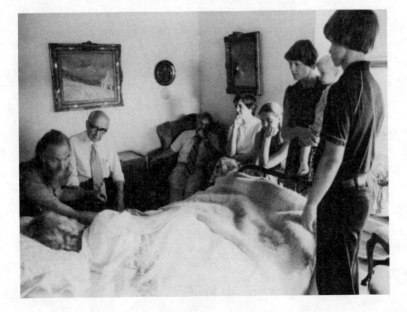

16 Sept. 9th, 1980, 20:30 Hours

9-10 September 1980
Ottawa

Last breaths.
Gasping life being extinguished.
Advancing chill of death.
Eyes unseeing.
"The LORD is my shepherd, I shall not want."
   Family gathered
   In red-eyed disbelief
   Numb.
"He makes me lie down in green pastures."
   Sobbing reality
   Too evident.
   Last washcloth for
   Your cooling brow.
"He leads me beside still waters; he restores my soul."
   Event ablur
   Time speeds or stops
   Faces streaked.
"He leads me in paths of righteousness for his name's
      sake."
   You heard the shepherd's psalm,
   Didn't you,
   Mother dear?
   For with its close there was
   Your multiplied deep sigh
   Head turned.
"Even though I walk through the valley of the shadow
      of death."
   Whispered messages of love

To unhearing (?) ears.
A hundred kisses.
"I fear no evil; for thou art with me."
Breathing stops.
Convulsive sigh.
Somewhere in the galaxies
A silent voice,
"It is finished."
"Thy rod and thy staff, they comfort me."
Frayed nerves accepted.
Prayers around the bed.
Time fragmented
Calm
The void.
"Thou preparest a table before me in the presence of
my enemies."
Stethescope
All is still.
She is gone.
"Thou anointest my head with oil, my cup overflows."
What? No vision?
No sense of presence?
No celestial choirs?
We cut a flower
And place it with her
—It only looks bizarre
Contrived!
No poetry here!
Just empty loss.
(And yet there is the awareness of steadying hands.)
"Surely goodness and mercy shall follow me
all the days of my life."
With them

I lift your body
To the stretcher
And that canvas
Womb.   —Face mottled
                    Children staring
                    Transfixed in grief.
"And I shall dwell."
  Tail lights of the hearse
  Grow smaller
  As they carry you away.
"In the house of the LORD forever."
Only the night remains.
Where are you, Mother?

17 Conversation

10 September 1980
Ottawa

Head bowed
Gasping sighs through bronchi constricted in protest.
　"I feel that I am standing at a precipice,"
　　　he said.
　"The cliffs to south and north,
　To east and west, are sheer.
　They drop a thousand feet
　To blackness."
"Do you feel that you will fall, Father?"
　"No.
　It is the view from Vimy Ridge.
　An outlook on
　Oblivion."

18 Wind of the Spirit

11 September 1980
Ottawa

And Jesus said to them,
  "When the Counselor comes,
  Whom I shall send to you from the Father,
  Even the Spirit of truth,
  Who proceeds from the Father,
  He will bear witness to me."

———————

When the day of Pentecost had come,
They were all together in one place.
And suddenly a sound came from heaven
Like the rush of a mighty wind,
And it filled all the house where they were sitting.

———————

The hours that followed your death, Mother,
Were hollowed with a dull knife.
But then, mercifully, they were filled
  with his presence.

———————

Did you see it?—God's sign.
Others went to work today,
Their world continuing.
Ours has stopped.
You there, sorrowing her loss, did you see it?
Did you understand?
You who knew her not, standing on the street corner
On your way to work.
Did you see it?
Comprehend?

The winds of God blew through this town today
A mighty wind from a brilliant, cloudless sky.
No storm. No barometric excuse. No thermal alteration.
Just the mighty wind.
                    Spirit with us.
                              His healing presence.
Hour after hour it came.
Cleansing all
Touching all you loved, Mother.
Surrounding us—fulfilling his command!
Passing through us
Uplifting.

———

Bless the LORD, O my soul!
O LORD my God, thou art very great!
Thou art clothed with honor and majesty,
Who ridest on the wings of the wind,
Who makest the winds thy messengers.

19 In Memoriam

12 September 1980: 1400 Hrs.
Dominion Chalmers Church
Ottawa

We gathered
Beneath the cross
Lives bound in common loss.

———

"I hope to see my pilot face to face
When I have crossed the bar."
We sang at your request
And knew your wish had been fulfilled.
"Blessed are those who mourn,
For they shall be comforted."
We were!
Dazzling sky bathed in brilliance

Proclaiming victory
An Easter of exploding light.

———————

In the tradition of the cross
We stood
In company with those who've gone before
Recipients of your healing love
        and his.
And in response, in joy, we sang:
   Thou art giving and forgiving,
   Ever blessing, ever blest,
   Well-spring of the joy of living,
   Ocean depth of happy rest!
   Thou our Father, Christ our brother,
   All who live in love are thine;
   Teach us how to love each other,
   Lift us to the joy divine.

20 37 Opeongo Road

12 September 1980
Ottawa

I felt this house weep today
In every room.
Thronging with people,
It vainly searched the faces passing through it, for your
    face.
Panelled walls,
The stairs,
Each corner turned
Provides
Another vista created by your hand.
There the spot where long you sat
Gazing at sailboats on the lake.
How much they meant to you!
"Like birds," you said.
And now, symbolically, that view o'ergrown with hedges.
Time obliterates each source of joy
        —sailboat view
          your smile
          yourself.
One source remains.

Love.

It feels so distant now.

21 The Green Bathroom

12 September 1980
37 Opeongo Rd.

Unsuspecting
I walked through the door.
I stepped into that room
And outside time.
Your presence overwhelms.
Not just yours—
    A thousand memories.
  In that sink you washed my hair...
  Too sick to go to school today...
  There's the Mitchell's house...
  Where is Pal?...
  Nettie will have the porridge made by now...
  While I sit here I'll review my part,
    The Lyres Club will sing next week...
  High school dance. Decorations were fantastic...
  Judy's chuckling laugh...
Bob, Dave, Pritch
El and Phyd...

———

Time shifts—
Same room
Peter slumps, fevered, toward the floor.
I catch him
And from unconsciousness
In whispered tones, he speaks,
   "Put me horizontal."
     —essence of Peter!

———

In this room
Your loving hands were never far away.
Can't focus.
Who placed this tourniquet around my throat?
Your absence overwhelms.
Reality rudely awakens
And screams the vacuum that is here.
Memories shattered.
The room weeps with me
In emptiness.

22 A Guide for the Winds of Change

14 September 1980
Ottawa

Deadener of the spark of life,
Heavy blanketing fog, crippling vision,
Depression settles
In the valleys of the mind.
It seeps through crevices
Into consciousness
Ensnaring the unwary lingering thought and
Confusing memory's path.

———————

He is bent with care.
Weighed down.
Senses crumbling.
His world shot through with emptiness.
Voyage interrupted—more than that.
For him she was rudder, keel and sail combined
   —all vanished.
"It is terrible.
Here I sit marking time.
Nothing left to do but wait my turn for death.
All purpose has departed!"

———————

Greyness.
The winds that now are blowing
Seem to bring
Only the chill of bleak despair.
They are the winds of change
That buffet us today
   —that buffet him.

All seems changed.
_____

We sail a foreign sea.
Depression's mists are gathering.
We need a guide, Lord.
A new course
To set our compass by.
_____

A voice speaks.
As to Israel of old
Isaiah calls to us
With prophetic sensitivity to the mind of God.
    Thus says the LORD,
    Your Redeemer, the Holy One of Israel.
        "Remember not the former things,
        Nor consider the things of old.
        Behold, I am doing a *new* thing;
        Now it springs forth,
        Do you not perceive it?
        I will make a way in the wilderness
        And rivers in the desert."
Lord, your words are apt enough.
We sail indeed a wilderness of soul,
A desert of despair.
Yet you promise a *new* way for us?
Even him?—aged as he is and bent with grief?
Again the voice.
    "I am doing a new thing for you.
    Now it springs forth!
    Do you not perceive it?
    Look not back,
    But set your course by me."
"But Lord, the winds of change, they overwhelm.

Uncharted are the seas that lie ahead."
The voice calls back.
   "Fear not, the new way
   Is *not* untried
   But established
   By my prophets and disciples long ago.
   Follow *their* example
   And set your course by me.
   For I am the way,
      the truth
      and
      the life."

Can it be that in this hour
We are called to open?
Not to close?
To set new sail?
God's promise stands
And aging ears must listen in faith
If they are to hear it.
God will do a new thing in your life, old man.
                                        In mine.
                                        In ours.

We must in faith reset our sails
And look not back.
Ever-present irony!
   Only in death do we find life.
   Only in turning from the past we wish so desperately
      to hold can it be ours.
   By setting our sites on a new star
   We build on the legacy she left us.
We must give up, to receive.

Empty, to be filled.

In our lives
As in our church
Tradition and expectant mission stand in tension.
The latter from the former born
Must always depart
If growth is to occur.
We must never fear
To set new sail,
To steer an unexpected course
When God's call is heard.

To sail from fogbound shoals
Into a brighter day
We need but heed the word from Butterfield:
  "Hold to Christ
  and for the rest

be
   totally uncommitted."
   ─────────

And through these mists
I see again your face, Mother.
Your plea to us
Is charged
With new meaning:
"Stand close to the Lord."
It is the word
By which we'll set our sails
To look for newness
   To serve,
   To open—to his plans.
And with new comprehension
We know
That you'll be standing with him
At our back.

23 Final Gift

27 September 1980
Ottawa

Discovering
  Integrating
    Accepting
  Separating
    Lifting
      Experiences
    Opening
      Emptying
        Centering
———————— Toward light
    Hope
   Joy.

24 Interment

27 September 1980
Ottawa

Final.
Final as
   Her name cut in cold stone
      A granite slab lying in the grass
        Wet,
            Stained,
                Bearing her name.
                   Her name!
Final as
   That square-cut
      Hole of blackness
        Yawning in the earth.
Final as
   A fine-grained polished box
      Of ashes.
Final as
   Figures huddled against the wind.
Final as
   An open book
   A preacher mouthing words.
Final as
   The emptiness that consumes
   The recognition that she has become
      Those chiseled letters
      Blurring from view
      In the chilling greyness
      Of this day.

25 Silent Voice

24 January 1981: 0200 Hrs.
Montreal

Lost youth
Face grown heavy with the passing years
Shadows ring the eyes.

Recognition—
    Peak passed!
    —Finite!—Me?—Yes!
—Why?
—Because, my friend.
"The circle game" Joni called it.
How many years ago was that?
They are all ablur now.
Where is Joni?
Where are you, Mother?
Hardly ever hear from either of you
These days!
But in my loss
I pause long enough to hear a voice.

———

The silent voice that bids us turn
From the rushing
    crushing
Maelstrom of our lives
Calls from within.
The doorway
To our inner selves
Is ours to open wide.
It opens to the light, the life,

the presence, the peace
That was always there.
In our essential aloneness
We are not alone.
For, as we open
We are filled
Losing self
To become
Other,
To become
One.

About the Author

Balfour M. Mount, F.R.C.S.(C), received his M.D. from Queen's University in Ontario and his training in surgery and urology at the Royal Victoria Hospital in Montreal. In 1968 he qualified as a urological surgeon. He has held a two-year fellowship at the Memorial Sloan Kettering Cancer Center in New York City as well as other fellowships including one at the Jackson Laboratory in Bar Harbor, Maine, where he did research on germinal tumors, and one at St. Christopher's Hospice in London. After conducting a study of the health care of the terminally ill at the Royal Victoria Hospital in the early 1970's, he established the McGill Palliative Care Service, where he now serves as director. He is also a professor of surgery at McGill University.